MUSICIANSHIP & SIGHT READING for GUITARISTS

To all my students past and present

Reprinted
March 1980
March 1981
September 1986
February 1990
January 1993
January 1994
July 1997
November 2001

MUSICIANSHIP & SIGHT READING for GUITARISTS

by Oliver Hunt

Index

CHAPTER I

Range	No higher than Position III
Key	No accidentals
Time Signatures	Crochet pulse
Texture	Single line
Note values	No shorter than crotchets
Test Example	Eight bars

CHAPTER II

Range	No higher than Position IV
Key	1 sharp
Time signatures	Crotchet pulse
Texture	Single line
Note values	No shorter than quavers
Test Example	Eight bars

CHAPTER III

Range	No higher than Position V
Key	1 sharp and 1 flat
Time Signatures	Crotchet pulse, quaver pulse and compound time
Texture	Two parts
Note Values	No shorter than quavers
Test Examples	Twelve bars

CHAPTER IV

Range	No higher than Position VIII
Key	2 sharps 1 flat
Time Signatures	Crotchet and quaver pulse (Compound)
Texture	Chords and arpeggios
Note Values	No shorter than semiquavers, and dotted notes
Test Examples	Twelve bars

CHAPTER V

Range	No higher than Position X
Key	3 sharps and 1 flat
Time Signatures	Crotchet and quaver pulse (compound)
Texture	Chords and arpeggios
Note values	No shorter than semiquavers and half beat rests
Test example	Sixteen bars.

CHAPTER VI

Range	No higher than position XII
Key	4 sharps, 1 flat
Time Signatures	Crotchet and quaver pulse (compound)
Texture	Chordal
Note Values	Syncopation, three quarter beat rests, duplets, and triplets
Test Example	Sixteen bars

CHAPTER VII

Range	No higher than Position XII
Key	4 sharps, 2 flats
Time Signatures	Crotchet, quaver and minim pulse
Texture	Chordal
Note values	Further syncopation, and triplets
Test Example	Twenty four bars

CHAPTER VIII

Range	No higher than Position XV
Key	4 sharps, 3 flats
Time Signatures	Signatures with odd numbers of beats
Texture	Chordal
Note values	No shorter than demi-semiquavers
Test example	Twenty four bars

CHAPTER IX

Range	Complete
Key	4 sharps, 4 flats
Time signatures	Changing time signatures with a common pulse
Texture	Chordal
Note Values	Triplets and quadruplets across the beat
Test Example	Thirty two bars.

CHAPTER X

Range	Complete
Key	5 sharps, 5 flats, atonal
Time signatures	Changing time signatures, with a changing pulse
Texture	Chordal, atonal, natural harmonics
Note values	Quintuplets, sextuplets, and septuplets.
Test Example	Forty bars

CHAPTER XI

Range	Complete
Key	6 sharps, 6 flats, atonal
Time signatures	Semiquaver pulse
Texture	Chordal, atonal, artificial harmonics
Note values	No shorter than semi-demi-semiquavers
Test Example	Twenty eight long bars

CHAPTER XII

Range	Complete
Key	7 sharps, 7 flats, atonal
Time signatures	Any, or any combination
Texture	Chordal, atonal, ornaments, and abbreviations
Note values	All irregular groups, Notes no shorter than demi-semi-demi-semiquavers
Test Example	Fifty bars.

MUSICIANSHIP AND SIGHT READING FOR GUITARISTS

By OLIVER HUNT
B.Mus. (Dunhelm).,L.G.S.M.,Hon.F.L.C.M.,

INTRODUCTION

This book has been written as part of a plan to broaden and integrate the various skills that are required from a guitarist in order to help him become a good all-round musician.

Teaching practice whether it be directed to the amateur or professional, places far too much emphasis on the performance of set pieces at the expense of such matters as sight reading, ear training and improvisation, which are given only scant treatment.

Good performing is of course of the utmost importance, and will be enhanced by the development of these other skills. Far too many guitarists think only of their techniques; - the shape of their nails, or what kind of strings they should use etc, as if consideration of these important parochial matters alone will be sufficient to turn them into good players. I have heard guitarists play with broken nails, appalling techniques, and rotten instruments, who somehow engage you by their sheer musicality, and make the instrument sing in a way that cannot be explained by technique. The simple answer is that they have music in them, which is largely due to the fact that they can hear as well as feel what they play. When most students play, they do not utilise their senses and other mental faculties nearly enough, and the fact that they are bogged down by technical difficulties often means that they are not hearing what they do, and no amount of hand exercises will improve this situation. It is therefore just as important to develop the ear and the mind, and to explore such matters as hearing and co-ordination in depth, which is also technique, but in a much broader sense.

This book concentrates on sight reading in conjunction with aural training. It is also concerned with co-ordination, and is designed to make the student far more aware of his fingers. The book is divided into twelve chapters which correspond very roughly with an average student's development from Grade I through various Diplomas to the fully fledged professional. Experience has taught me that there are certain aspects of sight reading which must be learnt systematically, and by so doing skill can be acquired far more rapidly than by haphazardly reading through vast amounts of music. These aspects may be summarised as follows:-

(1) Knowledge of the fingerboard.
(2) Knowledge of key signatures and the handling of accidentals within them.
(3) Knowledge of time signatures and rhythmic groups.
(4) The reading of both fingered and unfingered music.
(5) The reading of chords and arpeggios.
(6) The interpretation of expression marks.
(7) Learning to read ahead.

Since this is not a text on rudiments I have assumed in order to save space, that the student is familiar with them. It does however put knowledge of rudiments into practice, and if the student is not acquainted with them, there are many good text books which deal with such matters.

Before launching into the substance of this book I should also like to offer some advice on sight reading in general.

(1) Make sure that the side of the fingerboard is marked on the V,VII and IX frets, as these landmarks are of great assistance to begin with. I have also found that it is helpful for the guitarist to place the music stand on his left, which enables him to cut down the amount of head and eye movement, if he needs to look at his left hand before sliding into a new position. It is only the advanced player that can afford to do without these aids. There is therefore no stigma attached to using them.

(2) Since it is difficult for a beginner to read both accurately and in time, he should not try to do so at first. Instead he should deal with these problems separately as follows:- on the one hand reading out of time, working out note positions and fingerings before playing, and on the other, reading in time inaccurately if necessary leaving out or editing passages that cause difficulty. Both these approaches lead eventually to the art of reading ahead.

(3) Reading in the higher positions may be practised informally as follows:- If the top E string is not used, the student is compelled to think of alternative fingerings on those parts of the fingerboard which are not often used; a certain amount of editing may be necessary however.

(4) Familiarity with remote keys is best acquired by selective readings of music for other instruments, such as clarinet parts, or lute and keyboard music which necessitates a knowledge of bass clef.

(5) Alternative tunings such as (6) = D and (3) = F sharp, should only be practised when the student is thoroughly familiar with the normal tuning. It is not however necessary for him to select music written exclusively with these tunings in mind. Both the exercises in this book and guitar music in general will serve as practice material even if a certain amount of editing is necessary.

(6) Transposition should also be practised when the student has developed a degree of fluency in normal reading.

(7) Ensemble playing is a *sine qua non* for all guitarists, quite apart from the pleasure it gives, it helps the student to play in time and listen to the other performers.

(8) Last but not least, reading for pleasure. Taking a leaf out of the enthusiastic amateur's book, it is not a bad thing to read through pieces which are beyond the scope of the student provided that this is not over indulged, and that the music is not ploughed through in a slipshod manner. Many excellent though gifted sight readers have acquired their skill by this means alone.

Most students will ask how long they should spend practising these exercises and their sight reading in general. It is difficult to give an answer in round figures to such a question, but there are certain difficulties which should be recognised. The initial stages are by far the hardest, i.e. the problem of simultaneously counting, singing and playing which forms the basis of the practice method in this book. The initial stage should be taken slowly, at first spending about ten minutes per day on one or two exercises. As the student gains confidence, the time may be increased to half an hour a day. When the student can perform the examples in a particular chapter fluently and effortlessly the time may be reduced with a greater proportion of it spent on general sight reading. The accurate performance of irregular groups is another area where the time may have to be temporarily increased. Regular practice is vital, it is far better to spread it thin over a long period than to practise in fits and starts. Finally, I should like to pay tribute to Paul Hindemith whose Elementary Training for Musicians, was the inspiration behind this book, and to all my students both past and present, whose difficulties enabled me to come up with these solutions.

CHAPTER I
PITCH
Position I Scale

The practice method for Example 1 and similar ones in later sections is as follows:—

Call out the name of the note, the left hand finger, the right hand finger, then play the note. Calling out impresses information on the memory, gives more control and enables the student to learn more quickly.

Position I, note row with fingering

When the scale can be called out and played by heart, practice the note row in the same manner.

Position I, note row without fingering.

By this time the student should know where to find the notes, and which fingers to use.

Position I, sharps and flats.

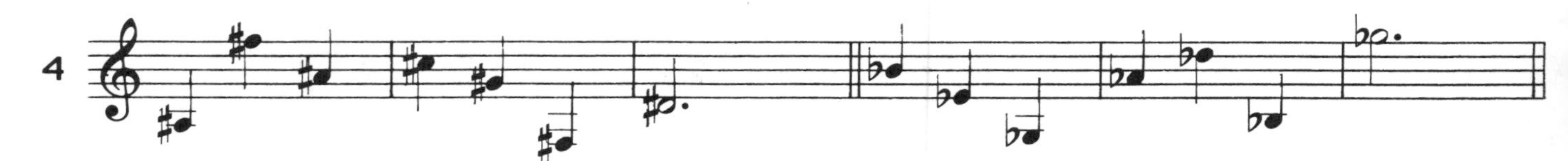

Practise the above sharps and flats which all lie under the hand

RHYTHM

In this rhythm exercise, all the main beats are counted out loud, and the notes are sung and played for their correct duration. The student should either play the bottom E string with the thumb, or the top E string with alternating i and m, taking care to damp the rests. The rests must also be counted, but with a normal speaking voice.

MELODY

The following fingered and unfingered melodies should be practised in a similar manner to the rhythm exercises, i.e. they must be sung, played and counted simultaneously. This method trains the ear as well as the hand and leads towards anticipating the sound of the music. It is also important at this stage to develop a high degree of awareness of both hands to ensure correct fingering. All fingered examples should be practised in the following ways. (1) Playing only. (2) Counting and playing, (3) Singing and playing (4) Counting, singing and playing, (5) Calling out right hand fingers, singing and playing (6) Calling out left hand fingers, singing and playing. By practising with this degree of rigour at the beginning stages all the essential foundations of hearing and co-ordination are laid, and much fruitless practice time is spared.

Position I

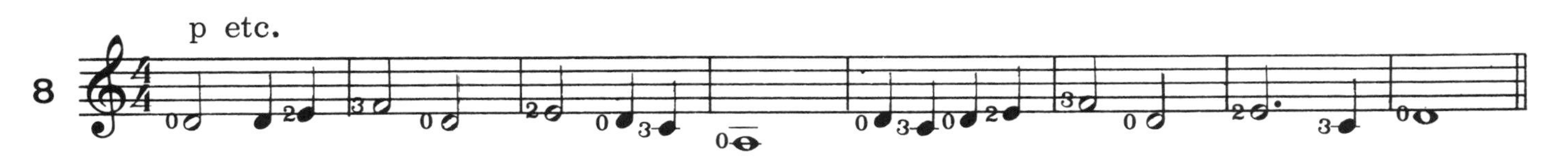

9
p etc.
10
m i m i m i m i m a m i m i m
11
a m a m i m i m i m i a m a m i m i a m
12
m i m a i m i m i m i m i m i m i m i
13
p etc.
14
p etc.
15
16

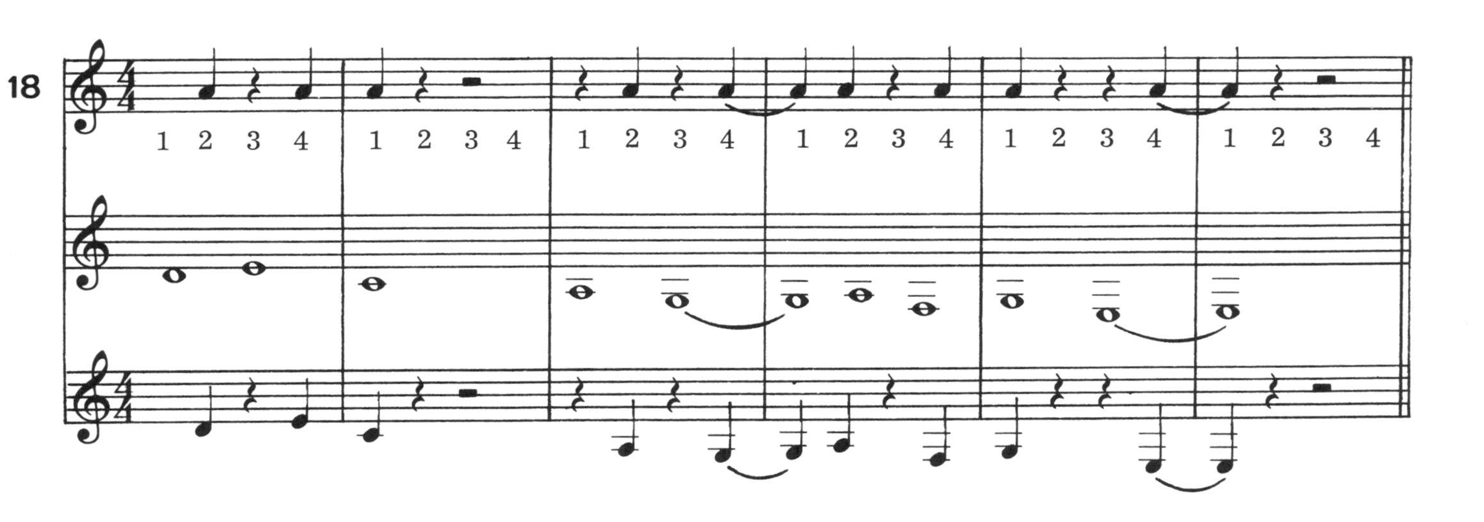

A beginner is bound to find it difficult to perform all these mental and physical gymnastics at once, and Example 18 shows how the problem may be broken down into constituent parts, which in themselves are easy. The first line represents the rhythm only, which should be practised first, the second, the pitches which may be performed in a free rhythm, and the third, the two combined to produce the original melody.

TEST EXAMPLE

Progress may be checked by reading the test examples at the end of each chapter. They should be performed in the normal way (i.e; without singing and counting etc.) but care should be taken to follow the expression marks.

CHAPTER II

The practice methods from now on are fundamentally the same as for Chapter I. In the rhythm exercises the verbal patter is placed underneath the notes and should therefore be self-explanatory.

PITCH

The above sharps and flats are all to be found on the fourth fret.

RHYTHM

24
p etc.
m i
m i m i m i m i m p etc.
25
i m i i m i m i m i m i a m i m i a m i m i
26
i m a m i m a m i m
m a m
27
28
29

30
31
32
33
TEST EXAMPLE
Allegro
34
i
m
m
a m
mf
i
a
m
m
a
m
i
m
i
rall.

CHAPTER III
PITCH
Position II Scale

In scales and note rows other than the first position, the fret on which the note is to be played is indicated by a roman numeral written above it and from now on it is the position rather than the left hand finger which should be called out.

Position II, Note row

RHYTHM

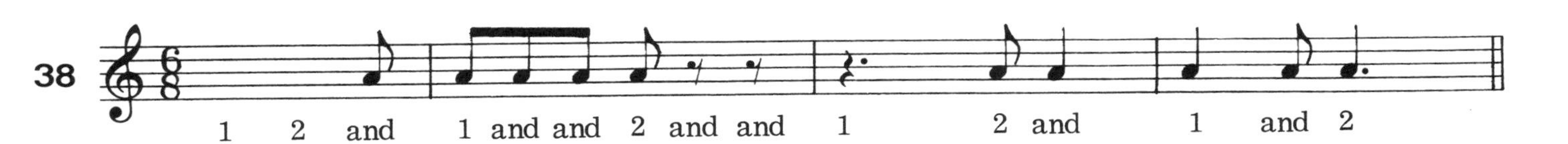

Compound times may be counted in two ways, depending on the tempo of the music. If it is at a slow or moderate pace, all six beats should be counted; and if it is fast it should be counted as two dotted crotchet beats each divisable by three as illustrated above.

MELODY

Position I

40
41
Position II
m i m a i m a i a m i m i m i m i
42
m i m i a m i m i m i m i m i
i m i m i m i m i m i m i m
43
i m i i m i m i m i m i m i m
44

TWO PARTS

In order to combine ear training and co-ordination, the following examples may be practised in a number of ways. (1) When two or more notes are played at the same time, it is best to establish the convention of reading from the bass upwards. This will eliminate mental dithering. (2) The top part may be practised in all the ways explained in Chapter I. (3) It is good practice to sing the bass line also. In all three cases both parts are played simultaneously which may cause a little difficulty at first, but it is excellent aural training.

TEST EXAMPLE

CHAPTER IV
PITCH
Position V, Scale

Position II
60
61
62
Position V
63
64

HARMONY

The following examples are in three or four parts, and enable the student to learn the fingerboard throughly. Here the emphasis is not on rhythm, and the counting procedures should be dropped. It is however excellent ear training to sing the inner parts as well as the bass and treble, taking each in turn. If the number of parts is inconsistent, the nearest note in another part may be sung as an alternative.

ARPEGGIOS

With this style of writing, singing should be dropped. It is very important however that the student learns to look ahead; the positions and fingers of the left hand must be found before the right hand is engaged, otherwise the result is utter confusion.

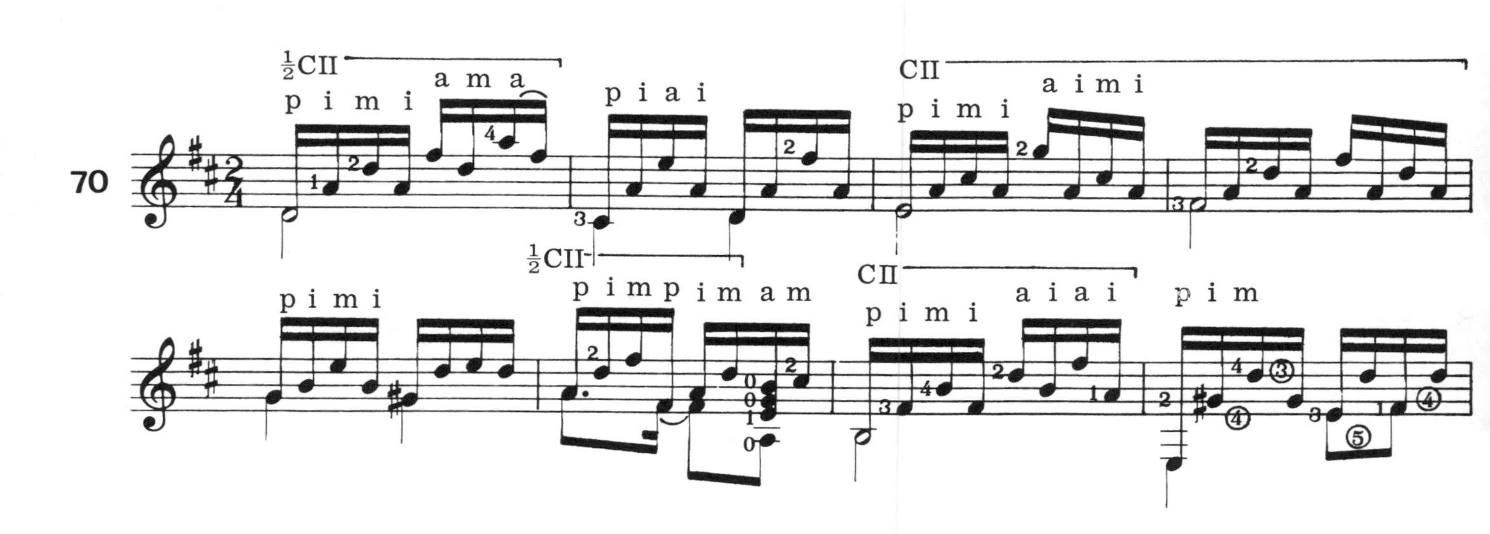

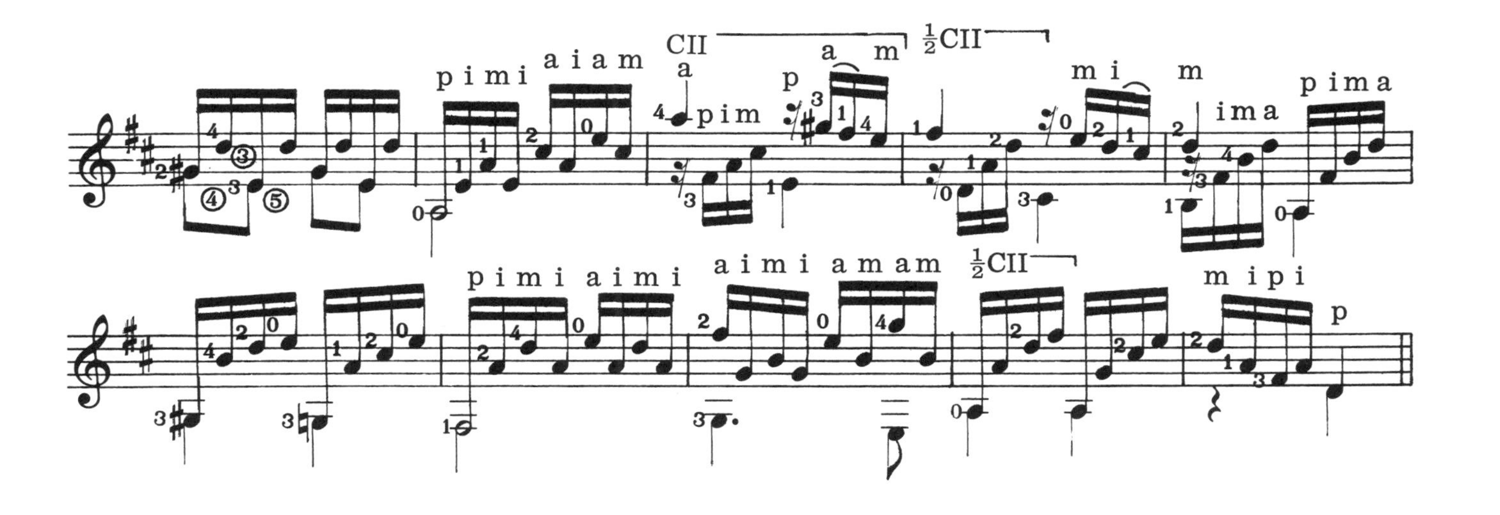

TEST EXAMPLE

CHAPTER V
PITCH
Position VII, Scale

80
Position IV
81
82
83
Position VII
84
85

86
87
HARMONY
CV
CVIII
CV
CVIII
88
CV
CVII
CVII
½CV
CVII
½CV
CV
CVII
CV
½CIII
89
CV
CIII

90
CVIII CV
CIII
CV
CVII
CV
CV
CV
91
½CVII
CVII
CVI
CVII
ARPEGGIOS
92
p i m
a
m i
a
i m

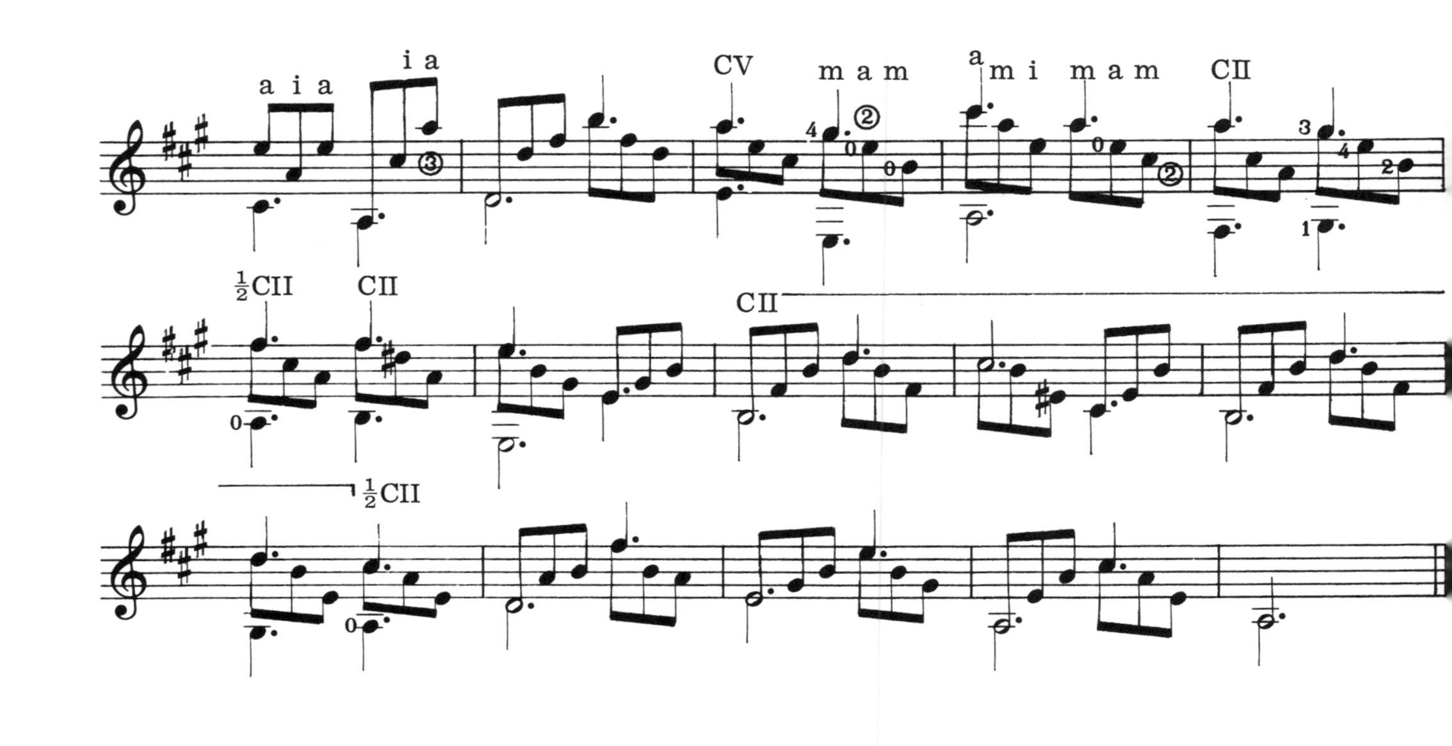

TEST EXAMPLE

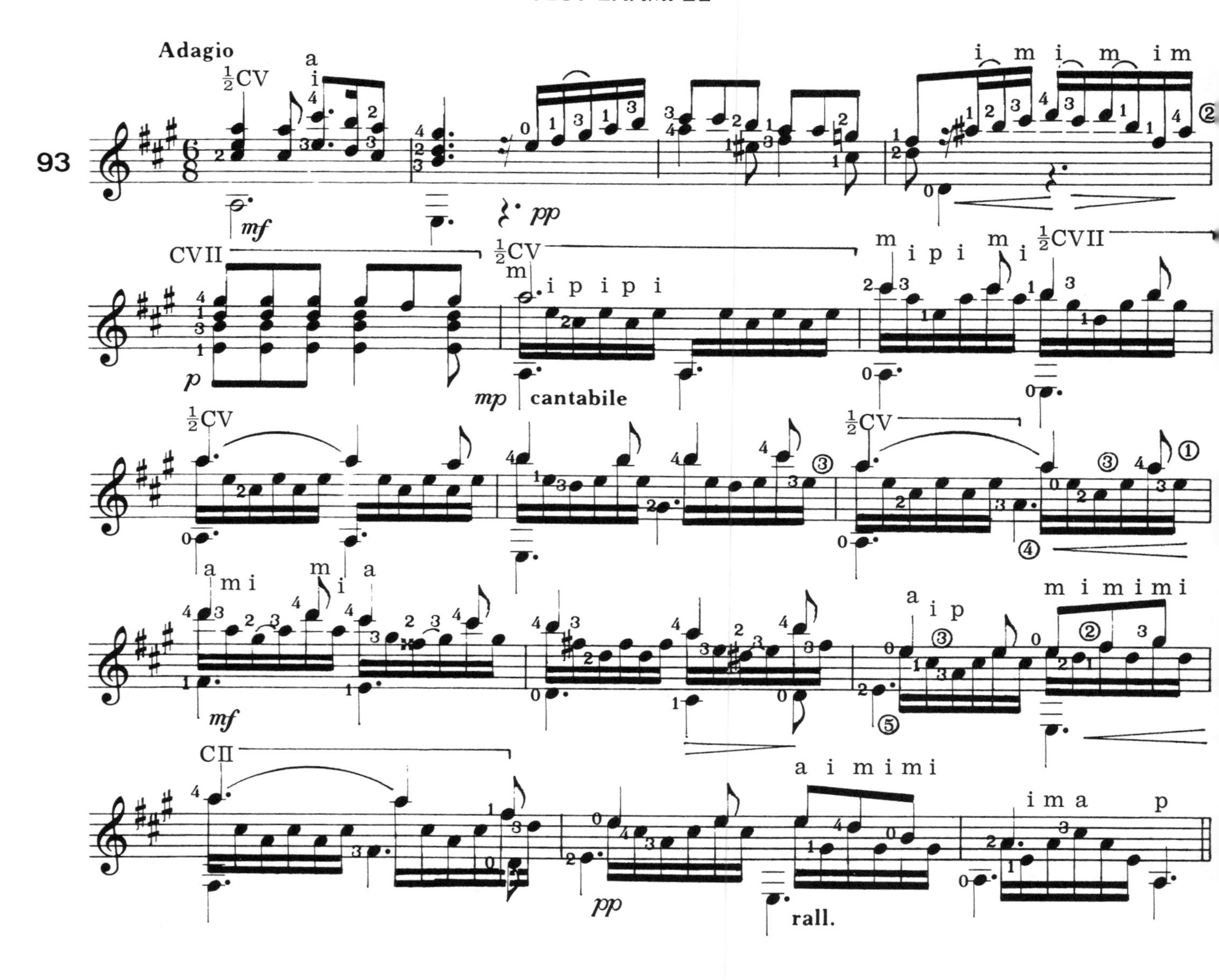

CHAPTER VI
PITCH
Position IX, Scale

Position IX, Note row

RHYTHM

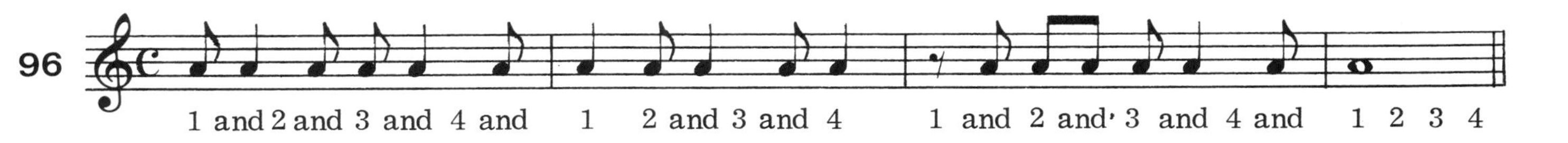

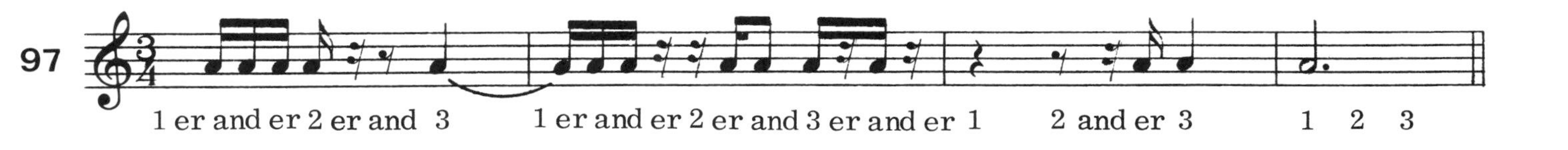

TRIPLETS

A former student of mine invented this ingenious verbal patter for triplets, and I have used it ever since. Care must be taken to space the notes evenly, and a steady beat must be maintained. If any difficulty is encountered a metronome may be of assistance.

DUPLETS

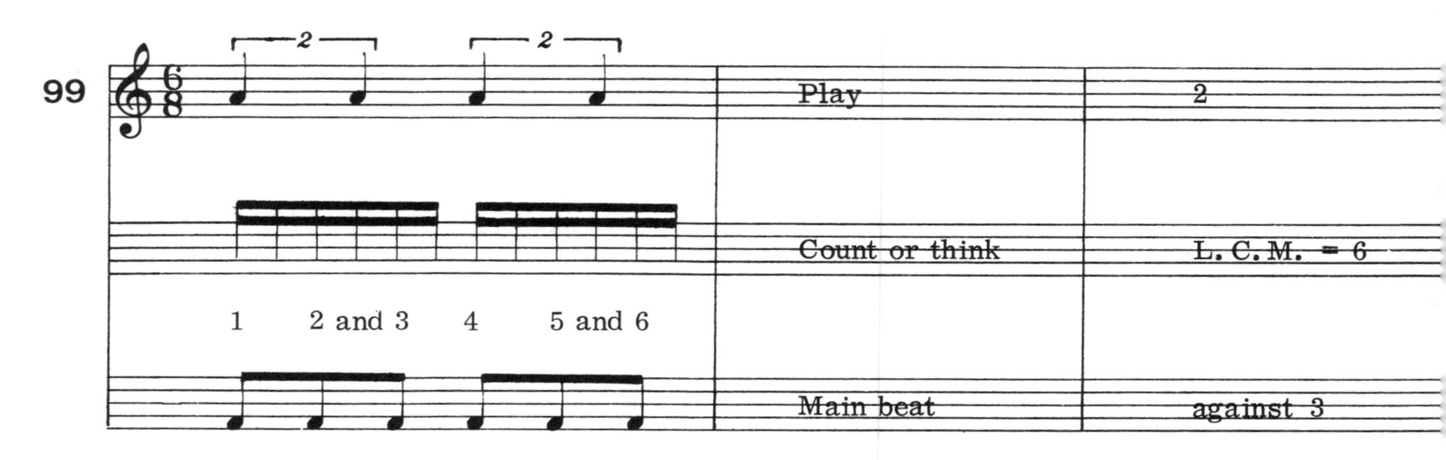

This exercise involves the problem of thinking across the beat, and I have devised this method to aid the student in spacing the notes correctly. With any irregular group, one must first find the lowest common multiple between the main beat and the group, and think of it mentally, while performing the latter against the former. Example 99 should make this clear.

MELODY
Position I

Position IV

109
HARMONY
110
½CX
CX
CVIII
CVII
111
CVII
CVIII
112
CVI

113
CVII
CX
CX
CIX
CIX
CVII
114
CIX
CVII
CVII
115
CIV
CII
CIV
CII
CIV
CVII
CIX
CIX
CIX
CVII
TEST EXAMPLE
Moderato
116
mf
½CII
CII
CVII
mf
CII

CII CIV
p
CII
CIV
CIII
CII
f
dim.
CII
CII
mf
rall.

CHAPTER VII
RHYTHM

MELODY
Position I

Position IV

HARMONY

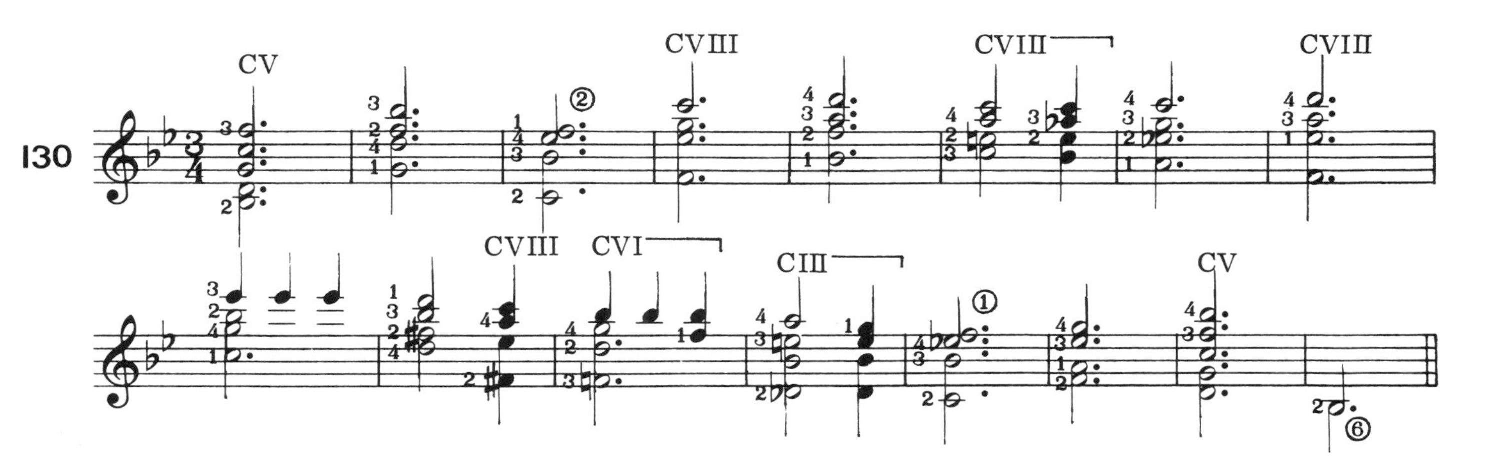

131
CIII
CV
CVI
CIII
CX
CX
132
CIX
CX
CVII
133
CII
CV
CVII
CII
CIX
CVII
CV
CIV
CIII
CII
½CII
CIV
CII
CIV
CII
½CII
CIV
CII
134
CII
CIV
CVIII
CVII
CIV
CII
CII

TEST EXAMPLE

CHAPTER VIII

PITCH

Since the first twelve frets complete an octave, it is easier both visually and mentally to think of positions XIII, XIV, XV and XVI as being positions, I, II,III and IV. The student should therefore call them out in this way.

Position XII scale

Position XII Note row

RHYTHM

By this time the student should have developed a sufficiently strong sense of rhythm to be able to dispense with some of the verbal patter. When the number of sub-divisions of the beat is large as it is in Ex 139, calling out every subdivision becomes an unwieldy task and is in danger of interrupting the flow of the music. With these examples and from now on it will only be necessary to call out the main beats; but if as in the case of Ex 139 the main beats are subdivided into many units calling out the half beat as well may be useful.

A propos of the above, I should like to make a comment about teaching practice in general. It seems that there are two schools of thought, apparently diametrically opposed, which are both trying to achieve the same end. One school works from the general to the particular, and the other from the particular to the general. The generalisers tend to think in larger units. The famous piano teacher Matthay believed that a good piano technique could be acquired by the use of various big gestures and arm movements, whereas the opposing schools based upon C.P.E. Bach believed that it could only be acquired by exercising the fingers individually. These opposing views can be extended much further and embrace one's whole musical outlook. In the case of rhythm, the Matthay school would encourage the student to think of a musical shape consisting of many smaller units as a whole. The C.P.E. Bach school would maintain that the larger shape could only be executed properly when the smaller units were thoroughly mastered; i.e, that if a phrase contained a smaller unit that consisted of a dotted crotchet followed by a quaver, and it was that latter part of it that caused difficulty, no amount of thinking of it as a whole would help the student to get the part right. So far it should be apparent to the student that I fall very much into the C.P.E. Bach camp, but this is not entirely the case, because I believe that both outlooks are valid, and it is more a question of the time that they are introduced rather than the fact that they are at loggerheads which is significant.

I believe that the detailed approach is valid for beginners, and that as soon as some degree of co-ordination, clear thinking, and hearing has been achieved, the student should gradually turn to the more generalised approach, when he really does have the skill and perception to think in larger units. The ability to do this will give his readings that breath of life which is the hallmark of a true musician. Anyone who has had experience of teaching beginners particularly if they have a small talent, will realise that the Matthay approach is far too exalted to be of much practical help.

MELODY

Position I
144
Position III
145
146
Position X
147
148
Position XII
149

150
Position XI
151
Position X
152
HARMONY
153
CXI
154

155
156
157
158
159
CVIII
CVIII
CVI
CVIII
CVI
CIII
½CI
CVIII
CIII
CI
CIII
CIII
½CIV
CI
CIII
CIV
CVIII
CVI
CVI
CIII CI
CIII
CIII CI
CIII
CV

TEST EXAMPLE

CHAPTER IX

PITCH

TRIPLETS AND QUADRUPLETS ACROSS THE BEAT

The practice method for these irregular groups is fundamentally the same as explained in Chapter VI, in each case the verbal patter or mental aid is given on the second line (see below)

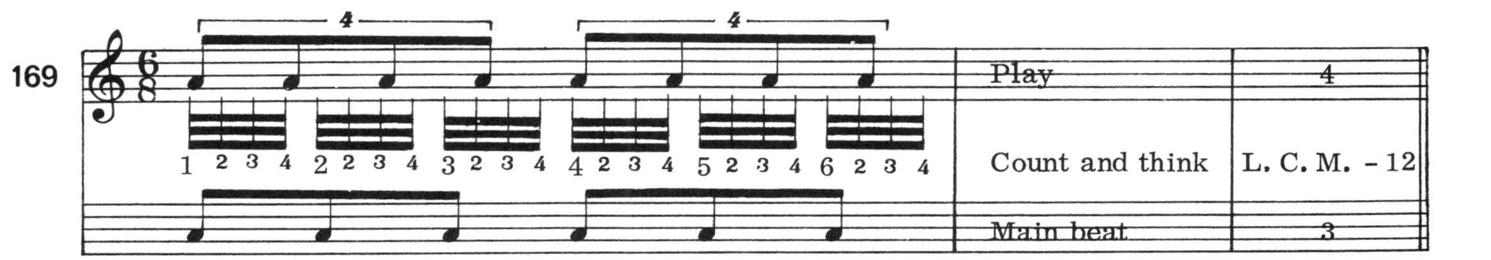

MELODY

Position III

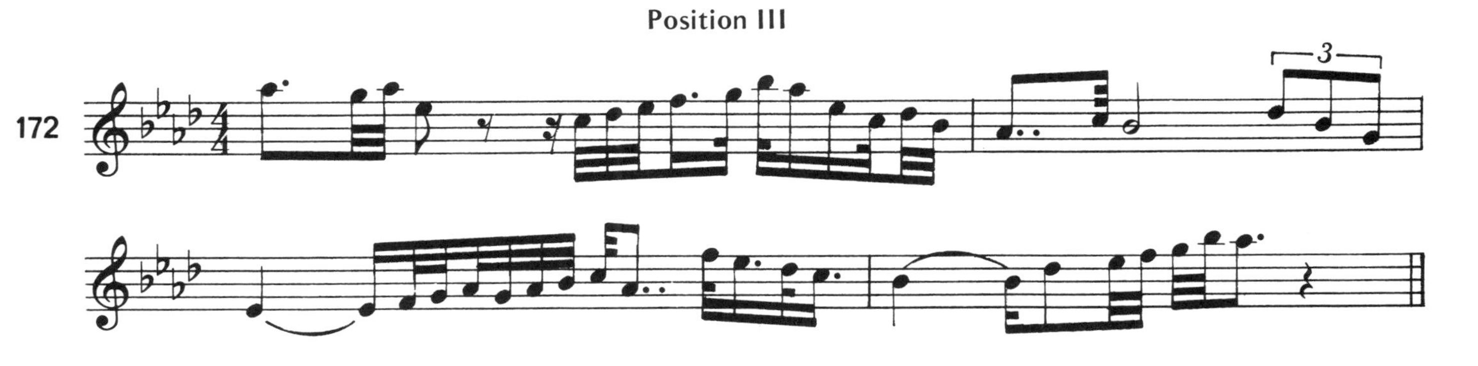

173
Position VIII
174
175
Position XIV
176
177
Position XV
178

Ex 178 and 179 consist of time signatures with a common pulse, but differing numbers of beats. This should cause no difficulty since the relative duration of the notes remains constant (i.e.; a crotchet in 5/4 has the same duration as a crochet in 4/4)

HARMONY

Some of the following examples are rather awkward to play but it is essential that the student should come to grips with the problem of reading and playing in high positions at this stage of his development.

182
CIV CIII CI CIII CVI
½CIV CIV CII CI CIV CVIII CVI
CVIII CIX
183
CXII
184
p i
185
CVIII CVIII

Vivace
186
½CV
½CX
CIII
CVIII
CVI
f
rall.
CIX
Arm12
a tempo
CVII
accel.
CI
p
CIII
mp a tempo
CV
CIX
meno mosso
CVII
CV
rall.

CHAPTER X

PITCH

Natural Harmonics

The reading of natural harmonics needs special attention due to the ambiguity of their notation. In some editions they are written as they sound (see the first line of Ex 187), but more often they are written as they should be played (see the second line of Ex 187, which shows all the alternative strings and positions which will produce one sound). In this example the notes and positions in the second line will produce the sounds written above them in the first line.

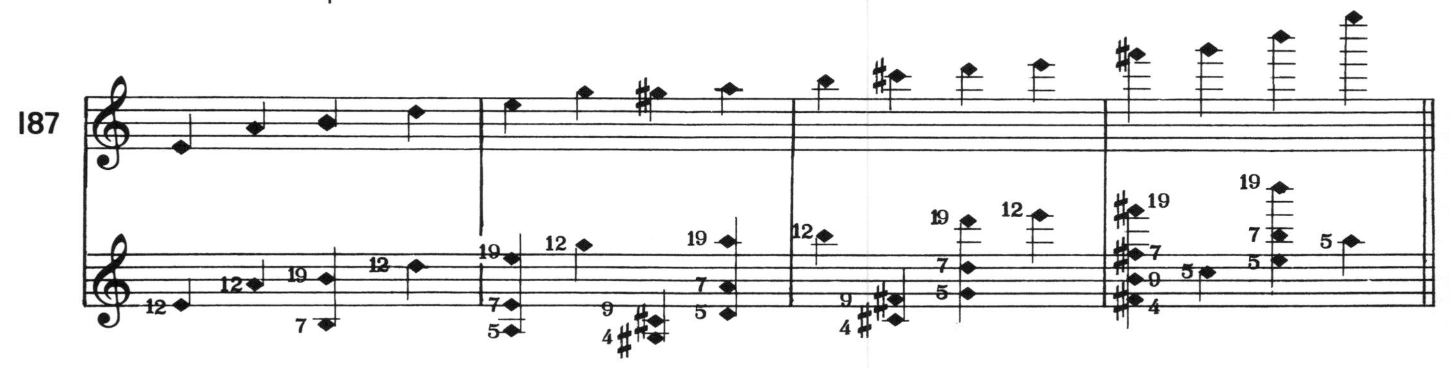

Note row of written harmonics

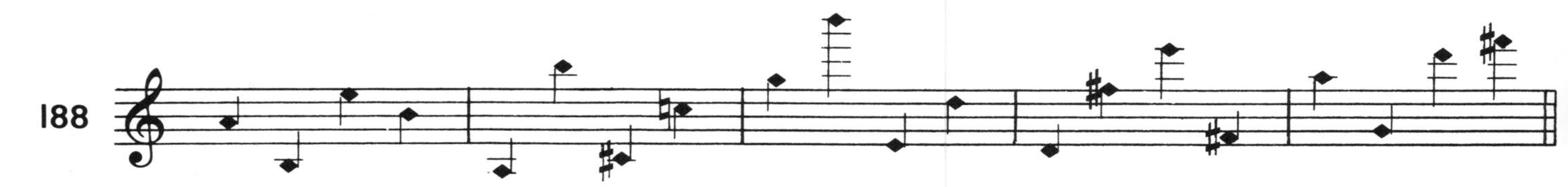

Note row of sounding harmonics

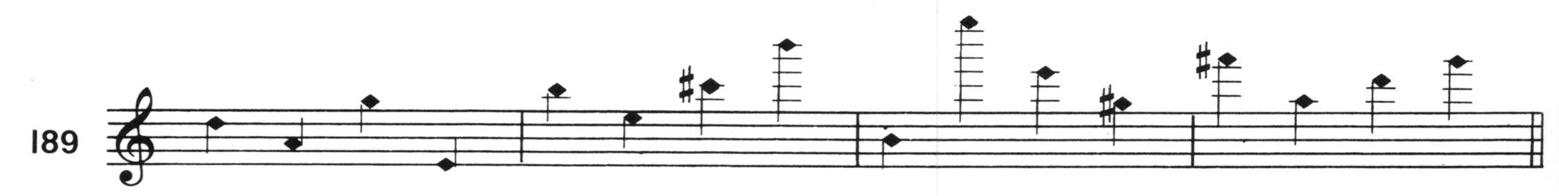

RHYTHM

In this chapter more common irregular groups are introduced; since none are across the beat, they should not present any difficulty, provided that the rhythmic pulse is strong and care is taken to space them accurately.

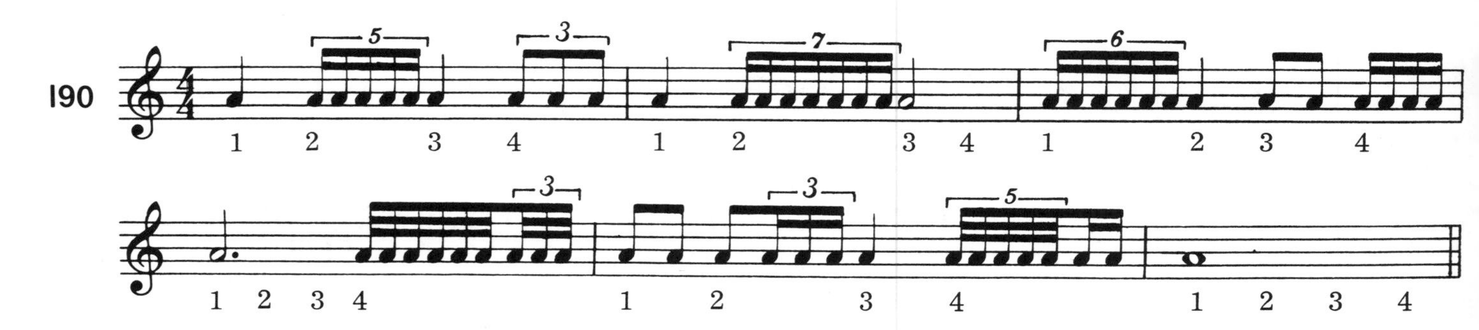

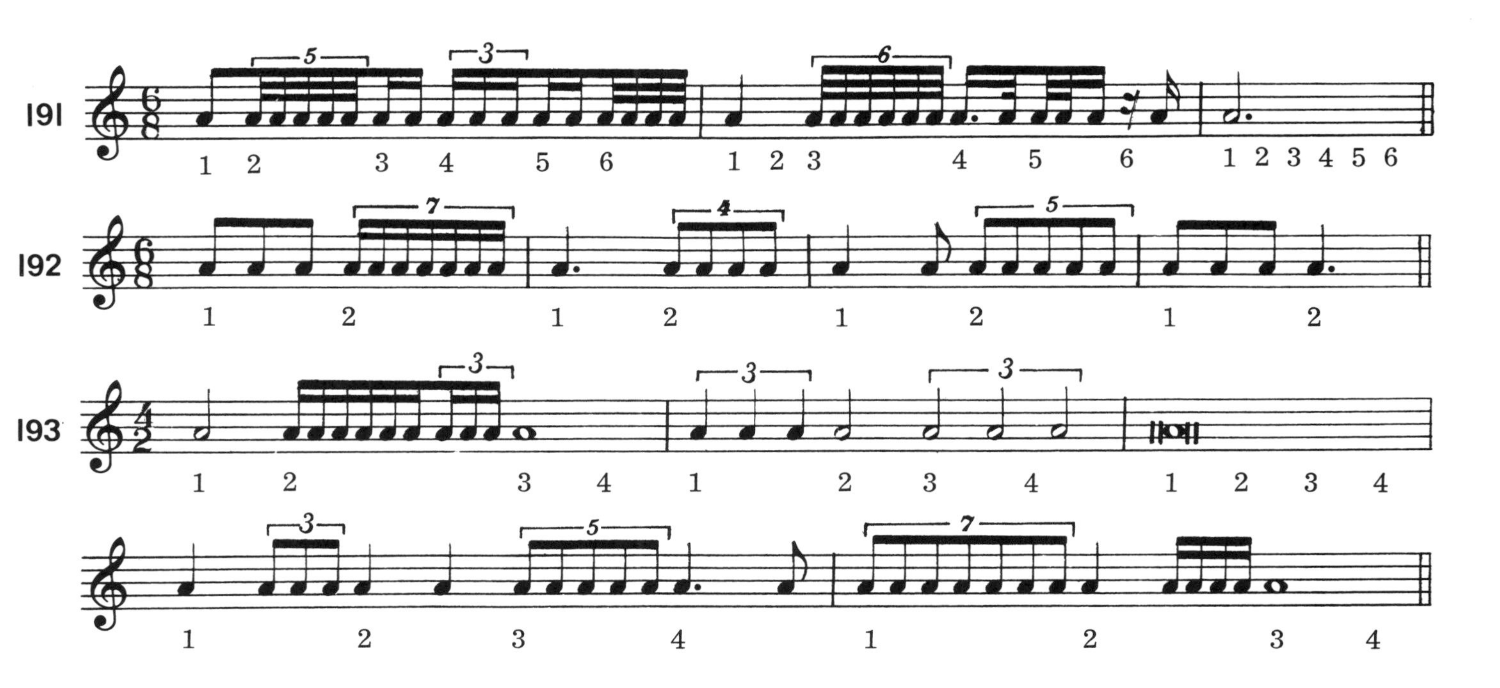

Changing Time Signatures

In these examples both the pulse and the number of beats change, but this still does not affect the relative duration of the notes (a quaver in 4/4 is the same length as a quaver in 6/8). In these cases the main beats and the smallest average units common to all time signatures should be counted, unless the student has a sufficiently strong sense of rhythm to dispense with such aids. The next two examples should make this clear.

MELODY

Position VI

Position VIII
198
199
Position XI
200
Position XIII
201
Natural Harmonics (written)
202
Natural Harmonics (sounding)
203

HARMONY

CVII CVI CIV CII CIV CVII CIV
204
CIV CIII CIV CVII
CVI CIII CIV CI CIV
205
CIV CVI CVIII CVII CVI
206
Arm. 12
½CI
CV

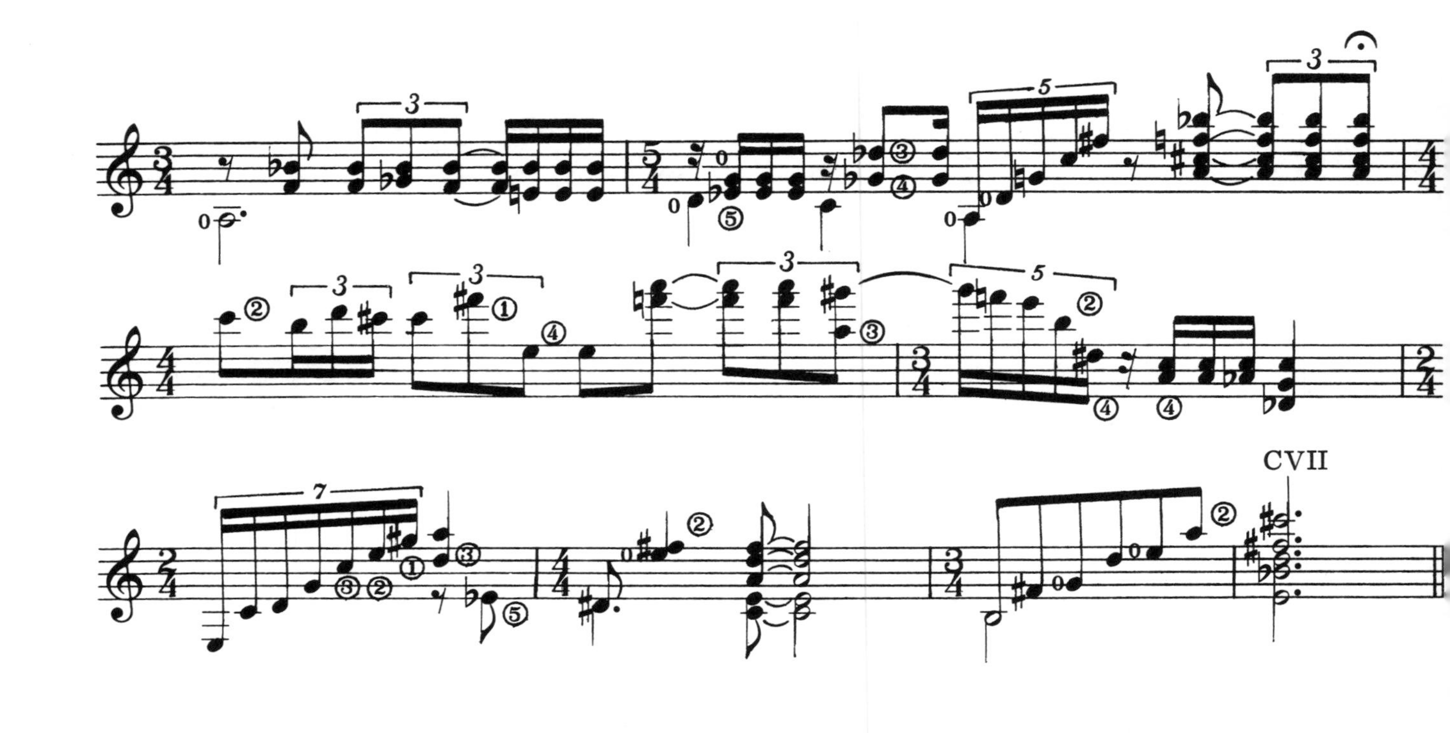

TEST EXAMPLE

CVII
CVIII
p
CVIII
CIX
CVIII
mp
dim.
rall.
p
tempo rubato
cresc.
cresc.
Arm. 19
mf
p
pp
a tempo
dim.
Morendo
pp

CHAPTER XI

MELODY

Position VI

Position I Artificial Harmonics

Artificial harmonics are always written at pitch, and therefore require no special comment.

CXI
CI
Art. harm.
Arm. 19
CV
Art. harm.
TEST EXAMPLE
Allegro
p a m i a m i a m i a m i a m i p i m a m a m i
217
mf
p a m i a m i a m i a m i a m i p i m a m a m i
p a m i a m i a m i a m i a m i
dim.
p a m i a m i a m i a m i a m i p i m a m a m i
mp

p a m i a m i a m i a m i a m i a m i p a m i
cresc.
p i m a m a m i p i m a m i p i p i m a m a m i
p a m i a m i a m i a m i a m i p i m a m a m i
p a m i a m i a m i a m i a m i p a m i p a m i p a m i p a m i
p a m i a m i a m i a m i a m i p a m i p a m i p a m i p a m i
p a m i a m i a m i a m i a m i p a m i i a m i m i a m i a m i
p i m a m a m i p a m i a m i a m i a m i a m i
dim.
p a m i a m i a m i a m i a m i
p
morendo
pp

CHAPTER XII

RHYTHM

Finally the most complex types of irregular group are introduced, and they fall broadly speaking into three categories. (1) All types of irregular group that go across the beat. (2) Irregular groups that are further subdivided or broken up. (3) a combination of both the above. Ex 218 illustrates how they may be simplified) for practice purposes. The top line is the part as it stands, and the second line shows how the groups may be either simplified by omission (the triplet), completed by insertion (the quintuplet) or regrouped (the nonuplet).

Irregular groups which go across the beat, and which have a greater number of notes than quadruplets are best felt rather than worked out arithmetically, because the L.C.M. is usually too large to be of any practical assistance. If a strong beat is established it should by this time be fairly easy to feel the group against the beat. In much contemporary music, particularly that of the late 50's to the late 60's irregular groups are employed so extensively that a more precise way of notating them has been devised. Eg. 5:4, 5:3, 7:6, where the first figure shows the irregular number of notes and the second shows the expected number of notes of the same type, i.e; 7:6 means seven semiquavers to be played instead of the expected six semiquavers.

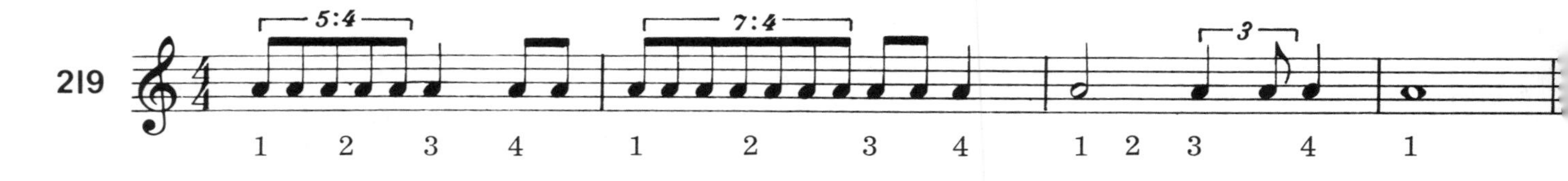

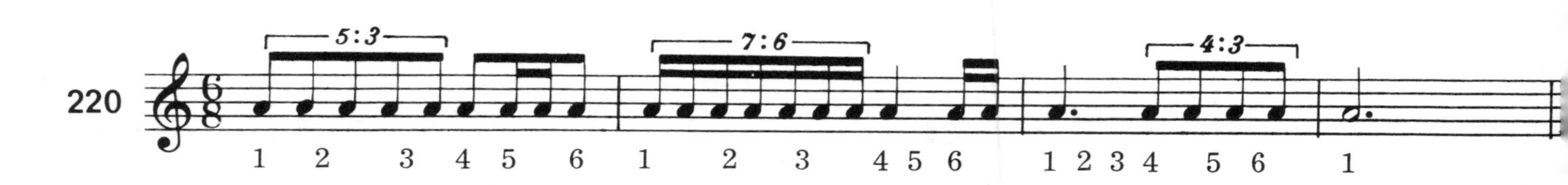

MELODY

Position VIII

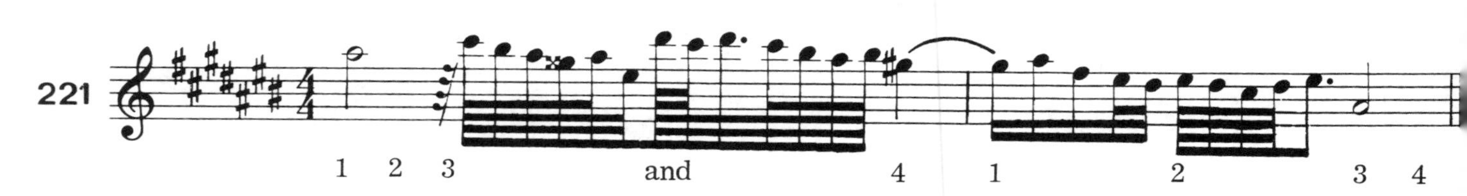

222
Position VI
223
224
Position XIII
225
Position XI
226
Atonal Melody employing irregular groups
227
228

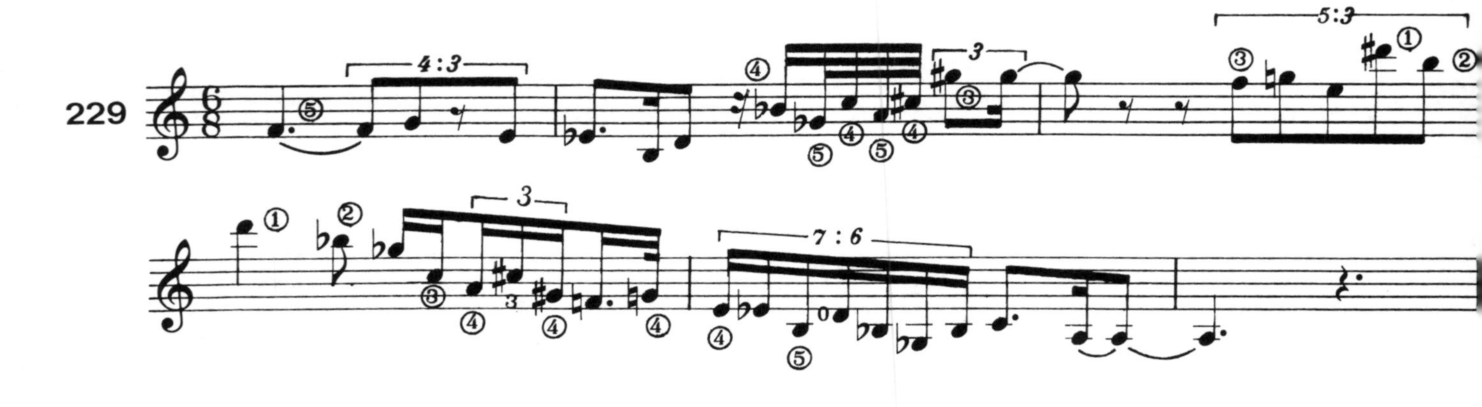

Abbreviations and Ornaments

For the sake of completeness I have included some rather frightful exercises in the realisation of the more conventional ornaments and abbreviations. Since this is not primarily a text book on ornaments, I have crammed as many as I could into as small a space as possible—the result cannot be musical!

TEST EXAMPLE

Printed and bound in Great Britain by
Caligraving Limited Thetford Norfolk

10/01 (41540)

CONCLUSION

I hope that this book will go a considerable way towards helping students with their sight reading problems. I must stress however that these exercises are a supplement and not a substitute for the reading of real music. It is possible however even with a book of this length to deal thoroughly with such matters as the general approach, rhythm, and the fingerboard; but short of writing the complete catalogue of existing guitar music it can only serve as a guide.